A Little Laughter... A Lotta Love

A Book Celebrating The Blessing of Moms

Inspired by Faith

A Little Laughter...A Lotta Love
©Product Concept Mfg., Inc.

A Little Laughter...A Lotta Love
ISBN 978-0-9895802-0-5

Published by Product Concept Mfg., Inc.
2175 N. Academy Circle #200, Colorado Springs, CO 80909

©2013 Product Concept Mfg., Inc. All rights reserved.

Written and Compiled by Vicki J. Kuyper
in association with Product Concept Mfg., Inc.

All scripture quotations are from the King James version
of the Bible unless otherwise noted.

Scriptures taken from the Holy Bible,
New International Version®, NIV®.
Copyright © 1973, 1978, 1984 by Biblica, Inc.™
Used by permission of Zondervan.
All rights reserved worldwide.
www.zondervan.com

Sayings not having a credit listed are contributed by writers
for Product Concept Mfg., Inc. or in a rare case,
the author is unknown.

All Rights Reserved. Except for brief quotes used in
reviews, articles, or other media, no part of this book
may be reproduced or transmitted in any form or by
any means, electronic or mechanical, including
photocopying, recording, or by information or
retrieval system, without permission by the publisher.

A Little Laughter... A Lotta Love

Mothers hold their children's hands for a short while, but their hearts forever.

Author Unknown

This book is dedicated to
mothers
everywhere, women who work tirelessly at a job that has no days off, no quitting time, no retirement plan and no paycheck... other than a lifetime of love. You're a blessing worth celebrating every day of the year!

Solo Competition

Motherhood is a competitive sport. We're always in competition with the mother in our head, the mom we want to be. But it feels like we're also in competition with every other mother throughout the annals of history. Especially the ones whose houses are spotless, kids are well-behaved and body fat ratio always falls on the skinny side of average. But no other mother since the dawn of time has faced what you've faced. Your family comes with its own unique joys and challenges. (Can I hear an "amen!")

So, it's time to stop competing against anyone other than yourself. Even then, give yourself a break! Even runners take a day off. Do the best you can with what you have today. Forgive yourself when you blow it. Learn from it. Then, move on. Regardless of how old your kids are, the race isn't over yet!

*Most of all the other
beautiful things in life
come by twos and threes,
by dozens and hundreds.
Plenty of roses, stars,
sunsets, rainbows,
brothers and sisters,
aunts and cousins,
but only one mother
in the whole world.*

        Kate Douglas Wiggin

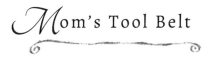om's Tool Belt

In every mother's tool belt, there are two indispensible items she needs each and every day: love and a sense of humor. Love sounds so obvious, almost cliché. But it's actually rather elusive, particularly because it's so difficult to bestow consistently. There are days when our kids are incredibly lovable. Other days, well...not so much. The same is true of us.

On those "other" days humor can help us through. Without love, humor easily slides into sarcasm. It bites instead of invoking belly laughs. It laughs at others, but refuses to poke fun at ourselves. Without love, it loses its effectiveness as a positive tool. But without humor, our love can subtly shift our role from nurturer to rule-keeper.

Love and humor, plain and simple, help us keep our kids (and the whole of life) in a more favorable light. So, slap on that tool belt and tackle today with a hug and a smile.

*A good laugh is sunshine
in a house.*

> William Makepeace Thackeray

*Give me a sense of humor, Lord,
Give me the grace to see a joke;
To get some happiness from life,
And pass it on to other folk.*

> Prayer from Chester Cathedral, UK

Laugh and grow strong.

> Ignatius of Loyola

Class Is In Session

There's been a movement among moms over the last couple of decades to seriously consider homeschooling their children. But the truth is, every mother does just that. Kids learn more at home than they will ever learn sitting at a desk somewhere else. They learn how to walk, talk, eat, play, pray and love. Those are lessons they will carry with them for the rest of their days.

So, be careful what you teach. Your example is their textbook. Your words, your attitudes, your habits, your outlook on life itself...your lesson plans are written by everything you do and say each day. Even if your children are grown, you're still teaching. You will remain one of the greatest influences on their lives. Let's keep that influence positive. It's good for the whole family!

*No influence is so powerful
as that of the mother.*

    Sarah Josepha Hale

The best academy, a mother's knee.

    James Russell Lowell

*One good mother is worth
a hundred schoolmasters.*

    George Herbert

*The bearing and training of a
child is woman's wisdom.*

    Lord Alfred Tennyson

*The future destiny of the child
is always the work of the mother.*

Napoleon Bonaparte

*My mother was the most
beautiful woman I ever saw.
All I am I owe to my mother.
I attribute all my success in life
to the moral, intellectual and
physical education I received from her.*

George Washington

*My mother was an
angel upon earth.*

John Quincy Adams

They Owe It All To Mom

Go ahead and admit it. It's all your fault. "What?" you may ask. Everything. If you're a mom, what your kids do as kids, as well as adults, seems to reflect solely on you and your abilities as a mother. Forget free will. When it comes to the court of public opinion, your kid succeeded because of your support or failed due to a lack thereof.

All we can do is our best—and hope we'll be the lucky ones, the ones whose children dedicate their Academy Awards, Olympic Medals and Nobel Peace Prizes to "my mother, without whom this would never have been possible." Okay. Maybe that dream is too lofty. Perhaps the best we can hope for is that if they do write a memoir about their childhood it won't become one of those bestselling ones about a terrible mother.

Famous Sons Wax Poetic About Their Moms

*If I am Thy child, O God,
it is because Thou gavest
me such a mother.*

Augustine

*In all my efforts to learn to read,
my mother shared fully my ambition
and sympathized with me and aided
me in every way she could. If I have
done anything in life worth attention,
I feel sure that I inherited the
disposition from my mother.*

Booker T. Washington

*All that I am or ever hope to be,
I owe to my angel Mother.*

Abraham Lincoln

*My mother was the making of me.
She was so true and so sure of me,
I felt that I had someone to live for—
someone I must not disappoint.
The memory of my mother will
always be a blessing to me.*

    Thomas Alva Edison

*I shall never forget my mother,
for it was she who planted
and nurtured the first seeds
of good within me.*

    Immanuel Kant

*She is my first, great love. She was
a wonderful, rare woman—you do
not know; as strong, and steadfast,
and generous as the sun. She could
be as swift as a white whiplash,
and as kind and gentle as warm rain,
and as steadfast as the irreducible
earth beneath us.*

D. H. Lawrence

Passport to New Pants

Let's put away all the lofty talk about the importance of child-rearing for a moment and take a look at a topic that is near and dear to every mother's heart: pants. Jeans, in particular. The presence of "mom jeans" in a mother's wardrobe has reached epidemic proportions. Yet, it's only a symptom of a deeper and more troubling problem. Mothers who have forgotten how to dress themselves...

We dress our kids. We dress our husbands. We dress the holiday turkey. But we neglect to dress ourselves appropriately and head out to the grocery store in an outfit that should have died along with disco. Somewhere in-between maternity clothes and polyester pantsuits there is a land of fashion. It's waiting for you. Dare to let your inner diva head out there and explore.

The Perfect Excuse

Mirror, mirror, go away!
These mommy jeans are here to stay...
Along with shoulder pads so tall,
And all my faded overalls,
Those plastic slip-ons for bad weather
And countless frumpy Christmas sweaters.
'Cuz my kids are so cute, you see,
That no one ever looks at me!

Vicki J. Kuyper

*Life is nothing but a series
of crosses for us mothers.*

    Colette

*A mother has, perhaps,
the hardest earthly lot;
and yet no mother worthy
of the name ever gave herself
thoroughly for her child who
did not feel that, after all,
she reaped what she had sown.*

    Henry Ward Beecher

*Oh what a power is motherhood, possessing
A potent spell
All women alike
Fight fiercely for a child.*

    Euripides

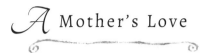 Mother's Love

Motherhood is like the ultimate blind date, one where it's love before first sight. Even before your child has had his or her "coming out party," you know you'd do anything for that itty-bitty kid. Maybe, it's because you already have...

When you were pregnant, you cut out caffeine. You tried to eat healthy. You wore clothing that really can't be classified as fashion forward. You put up with heartburn and back aches and Braxton Hicks. Then, you go through labor. Now, that's love! Have faith. One of these days, your love will be reciprocated with a bouquet of flowers on Mother's Day—shortly after your children have children of their own.

What's In a Name?

As mothers, we have power. The question is, will we use that power for the positive or negative? One not-so-subtle clue is the name we choose to bestow upon a tiny, innocent baby. After all, the moniker we choose will likely be what people use, or abuse, when referring to our beloved child for the rest of his or her days. In other words, we'd do well to choose carefully.

But, there's so much to consider! Does it lend itself to any embarrassing nicknames? Does it fit a two-year-old, but not an adult—or vice-versa? Will the initials spell out an undesirable word on monogrammed luggage? Just keep in mind that your children get to choose your "grandparent" nickname once they have kids of their own. Payback could transform you from Grandma into "Goo Gum," if you're not careful.

*A name is a kind of face
whereby one is known.*

> Thomas Fuller

*Words do not change their
meanings so drastically in the
course of centuries as, in our minds,
names do in the course of a year or two.*

> Marcel Proust

*Our names are labels,
plainly printed on the
bottled essence of our
past behaviour.*

> Logan Pearsall Smith

*It only seems as if you're doing
Something when you're worrying.*

    Lucy Maud Montgomery

*See to it that your boys and girls,
when they grow up, do not remember
you as an anxious, worried,
irritable mother; but live such a
trustful life before them that they
will have always a picture of peace
and trust when they think of you.*

    Hannah Whitall Smith

*Worry often gives small things
a big shadow.*

    Proverb

In a Maternal Stew

Every mom knows that kick in the gut that starts during pregnancy—and we're not talking about embryonic gymnastics in utero. We're talking worry. Those anxious thoughts that weigh so heavily on our hearts, that desperate bargain of a prayer where we'd give anything if we could just ensure the health and happiness of our kids.

Worry doesn't "care" for our children. It simply robs us of peace and joy. If left unchecked, our fretting can become as much of a burden to our kids as it is to us. Like literal nail biting, it's a habit that needs to be broken. So, when anxious thoughts begin, picture each individual worry as a helium balloon. Then, let it go. We can't control circumstances. But we can offer encouraging words, a helping hand and a heartfelt prayer. Being positive and proactive does more good than fussing and fretting ever will.

"Other" Mothers

Not all mothers come to us at birth. Some we're blessed enough to discover along the twisty road of life. We may, or may not, be related by blood. But that's of little consequence. It's love—not biology—that truly transforms a woman into a mother.

At first, we may know her by another title, such as aunt, grandmother, neighbor, mentor…or simply friend. But then she becomes more. Her influence on us is foundational. Her love for us, unshakeable. When we look back on our lives, we have her to thank for helping us become the person we are today. "Other" mothers are a blessing not everyone receives. That makes them even more precious, and more worthy of celebrating, when they happen to come our way.

*At times our own light goes out
and is rekindled by a spark from
another person. Each of us has cause
to think with deep gratitude of those
who have lighted the flame within us.*

Albert Schweitzer

*Our chief want in life is somebody
who shall make us do what we can.*

Ralph Waldo Emerson

*All love is sweet, Given or returned.
Common as light is love,
And its familiar voice wearies not ever.*

Percy Bysshe Shelley

The Power of Praise

In households all over the world, there's a recurring scenario that strikes fear into the heart of every mom...It begins when you're busy, preoccupied with accomplishing one of the tasks you should have done yesterday. You notice the house is quiet. Too quiet. You call out your toddler's name. There's no response.

As you hurry down the hall, you notice an open desk drawer. Markers litter the floor. Permanent markers. That's when you hear those dreaded words, announced with such pleasure and pride: "Mommy! Look what I did!"

Yes, your pint-sized Picasso has struck again.

If you're lucky, your child has used the wallpaper you've always hated as his canvas. More likely, it's that freshly-painted hallway, newly laid bathroom tile or recently varnished baseboard. Kids know quality materials when they see them.

Of course, we encourage it. What do we do when Little Jenny or Jeremy puts a few random crayon marks on paper and asks how we like the "doggie"? We tell them what amazing artists they are! We "ooohh" and "aaahh." We brag about their artwork to the grandparents. Then, we hang it on the fridge. With positive reinforcement like that, it's surprising there are any flat surfaces in our home left unmarred.

Think about it. Maybe that's how Picasso really got his start. He was scribbling away on the kitchen wall when his loving mother, trying not to hurt his feelings or stunt his creative growth, said with a smile, "Oh, Pablo! It's wonderful. Yes, that big cube looks just like your sister's head! And I love the way you have her foot growing right out of her armpit. It's so colorful. So creative. You're a genius!"

The rest is history.

*Every child is an artist.
The problem is how to remain
an artist once we grow up.*

Pablo Picasso

*If children grew up according
to early indications, we should
have nothing but geniuses.*

Johann Wolfgang von Goethe

*A child is not a vase to be filled,
but a fire to be lit.*

François Rabelais

*When children are doing nothing,
they are doing mischief.*
> Henry Fielding

*The soul without imagination is
what an observatory would be
without a telescope.*
> Henry Ward Beecher

*A mother's children are like ideas;
none are as wonderful as her own.*
> Proverb

More Than Meets the Eye

You're a mother! Who wouldn't want to brag about a title like that? But you are more than "just" a mom. You were someone of value before you took on that role, a woman with her own genetic crazy quilt of talents, personality and potential.

Amidst the potty training, soccer schedules, housecleaning and steering your children on a steady course to, and through, adulthood, it can be easy to lose sight of that fact. But there's more to your life than just counting the seconds until you can add "Grandma" to your name. Or, at least, there should be. There's a life story outside of and apart from your children's. Don't miss out on it! Choose to see yourself with the same promise of possibility as you view your kids. Just like them, you're still growing. Who knows who you'll grow up to be!

*What is truly indispensable for the
conduct of life has been taught us
by women—the small rules of courtesy,
the actions that win us the warmth
or deference of others; the words that
assure us a welcome; the attitudes
that must be varied to mesh with
character or situation; all social strategy.*

    Remy de Gourmont

Growth is the only evidence of life.

    John Henry Newman

*It is right to be contented with
what we have, but never with
what we are.*

Sir James Mackintosh

*There is just one life for
each of us: our own.*

Euripides

*We have no power to fashion
our children as suits our fancy;
As they are given by God,
we so must have them and love them;
Teach them as best we can, and let
each of them follow his nature.
One will have talents of one sort,
and different talents another.
Every one uses his own, in his own
individual fashion.*

Johann Wolfgang von Goethe

One Life Per Person

Having a child can feel like a second chance... To go to the prom. To be beautiful. To get chosen for the team. To make our mark on the world. To watch our dreams come true. But make no mistake: our kids are individuals. They have their own life stories to write, complete with all of their own successes and failures.

Living vicariously through our kids doesn't do justice to anyone. It's fantasy, not reality. It keeps us, as moms, from fully experiencing today through our own eyes. And it diminishes the significance, and singular journey, of the amazing children we have the privilege of sending off into the wilds of adulthood.

Children need breathing room to live their own lives and become the individuals they were created to be. The same is true for us moms. Just like half-baked brownies, neither of us are done yet!

Every toy left on the floor,
Each smudge of dirt found on the door,
Or shattered shard of broken vase,
Can't wield the power to erase
The joy I've found in disarray,
Because I've taken time to play
With someone who's sweet, tiny smile
Reminds me how to be a child.

Vicki J. Kuyper

Welcome to Wonder

Kids are pint-sized Einsteins when it comes to teaching Mom a thing or two. Like how to play. How to belly laugh. How to have so much fun you lose track of time. How to let go of a grudge. How to care less about what you're wearing. How to let your imagination take you on a wild ride.

To kids, there are no ordinary days. Only extraordinary ones. Each new day is a kind of wonderland where magic, miracles and fairy tales just may come true. As adults, we often look down on their "faith" as out of touch with reality. But perhaps they know something we've forgotten. We never know what today may hold—and just because something has never happened before, doesn't mean it never will.

*A man can stand almost anything
except a succession of ordinary days.*

Johann Wolfgang von Goethe

*Each day is a little life;
every waking and rising a little birth;
every fresh morning a little youth.*

Arthur Schopenhauer

*The soul is healed by
being with children.*

Fyodor Dostoyevsky

*Speech is external thought,
and thought internal speech.*

    Antoine de Rivarol

*Like a forgotten fire, a childhood
can always flare up again within us.*

    Gaston Bachelard

*There are only two ways to live
your life. One is as though nothing
is a miracle. The other is as though
everything is a miracle.*

    Albert Einstein

A Good Word

A mother's words pack a powerful echo. Our children are likely to live up to, or down to, the verbal picture we paint of them on a daily basis. That means we need to choose our adjectives carefully. If we tell them they're sharp-as-a-whip, cute-as-a-button and oh-so-loved in lots of little ways throughout their lifetimes, they will be more apt to see themselves that way. If we imply they're dimwitted, an imposition or a perpetual troublemaker, they'll likely see themselves through those negative lenses just as easily.

We don't need to lie to our kids by assuring them they're all geniuses and virtuosos. But we do need to help them discover the true beauty and blessing hidden in each one of them. Let our words serve as a magnifying glass that helps uncover and encourage the very best in our kids—as well as everyone we meet.

*The only way to speak the
truth is to speak lovingly.*

Henry David Thoreau

>
> *Correction does much,
> but encouragement does more.*
>
> Johann Wolfgang von Goethe

*Education commences at the
mother's knee, and every word
spoken within the hearing of
little children tends towards
the formation of character.*

Hosea Ballou

> *I can live for two months
> on a good compliment.*
>
> Mark Twain

The Baby Book Blues

When your first child is born it's like the world has been created anew. You document every moment. First smile. First haircut. First word. First steps. You turn imprints of tiny hands into plaques and immortalize pigeon-toed footprints on stepping-stones.

While the baby's asleep, you're hard at work recording baby's next breath. The album you're creating rivals the family Bible in size. Every page is a masterpiece, bordered in hand-cut hearts. Your glue stick budget rivals that of disposable diapers. Along comes Kid Number Two. You buy the album. But the photos remain in stacks right next to it on the shelf. Occasionally, you jot dates on the photo envelopes so you'll remember all of those firsts. You'll record them somewhere permanent when you have time. Like when the kids are in college.

Welcome Kid Number Three. Who needs an album? You have photos. On your phone. One day you'll learn how to download them. Of course, you do have that ultrasound tucked away. Or is that the X-ray of your gall bladder? Whatever. You can't even remember if you actually sent out those birth announcements. If not, relatives will probably catch on by the time the graduation announcements arrive.

And if you have more than three children, or had them arrive in multiples, if you actually have a photographic record of any kind AND can still tell your kids' baby pictures apart, you should be a shoe-in for sainthood.

But here's the really good news. Albums are old school. Pages have gone virtual. So, consider social media your new baby book. If your kids demand a tangible record, print anything you've posted. Staple everything together and voilà! Baby Book! Sure, the kids may mutter under their breath about your inadequacies as a mother. But, only until they have kids of their own.

A baby will make love stronger,
days shorter, nights longer,
bankroll smaller, home happier,
clothes shabbier, the past forgotten
and the future worth living for.

Pablo Picasso

Every child born into the world
is a new thought of God,
an ever-fresh and radiant possibility.

Kate Douglas Wiggin

It seems a breath from heaven
Round many a cradle lies,
And every little baby
Is a message from the skies.

Frances E. W. Harper

The family is like a book—
The children are the leaves,
The parents are the covers
That protecting beauty gives.
At first the pages of the book
Are blank and purely fair,
But Time soon writeth memories
And painteth pictures there.

    Author Unknown

A Word to the "Whys"

For mothers, storytime isn't reserved for bedtime. Sometimes, we have to make-up fairy tales on the fly. Like when our 3-year-old asks, "Where do babies come from?" or our teen inquires (with a brand new set of car keys in hand), "Don't you trust me?" Yes, there are plenty of things we mothers say that wouldn't hold up under the scrutiny of a lie detector test.

We work hard to not discourage our kids or scar them for life with the cold, hard truth. But we can't step too far away from reality. Our kids need to know our words can be trusted. We can be thoughtful, tactful and age-appropriate when tackling tough subjects with our kids. But we also need to be real. The more honest and authentic we are with our words, the more likely our children are to follow in our verbal footsteps.

*No man means all he says,
and yet very few say all they mean,
for words are slippery and thought
is viscous.*

    Henry Adams

*Is it true; is it kind,
or is it necessary?*

    Socrates

*If you tell the truth, you don't
have to remember anything.*

    Mark Twain

Pass It On

A legacy is what we leave, a heritage... what we've received. We do our best to help point our kids in the right direction, to give them the tools they need to help get them where they want to go. But there's one tool all too often ignored: the knowledge of where they've come from. We're not talking about the birds and the bees. We're talking about the roots of our family tree. There was a story going on before our children entered this world, one that continues beyond our generation, and theirs. The more our kids identify with this story, the more they'll feel a part of something bigger than themselves.

Talk about nationality, race, religion, relatives, traditions...even old family recipes. Tell stories. Check out old photos. Do some genealogical research. Uncover some roots together. So often, kids puzzle over their identity. Why allow family history to be a missing piece?

*In a brief space the generations of
beings are changed, and, like runners,
pass on the torches of life.*

    Lucretius

*My great grandfather used to say
to his wife, my great-grandmother,
who in turn told her daughter,
my grandmother, who repeated it to
her daughter, my mother, who used to
remind her daughter, my own sister,
that to talk well and eloquently was
a very great art, but that an equally
great one was to know the right
moment to stop.*

    Wolfgang Amadeus Mozart

*There is properly no history,
only biography.*

    Ralph Waldo Emerson

The Day You Were Born...

Only a baby small,
Dropped from the skies;
Only a laughing face,
Two sunny eyes.
Only two cherry lips,
One chubby nose,
Only two little hands,
Ten little toes.

Only a tender flower,
Sent us to rear.
Only a life to love,
While we are here.
Only a baby small,
Never at rest,
Small, but how dear to us,
God knoweth best.

    Matthias Barr

Playing It Safe

Back in the dark ages when we were kids, we danced with danger. Forget about being buckled into kids' car seats. We didn't even have seatbelts.

When playtime came around, our favorite toys included kid-friendly items like wood burning kits, BB guns, chemistry sets, and Swiss army knives. Back then, when Mom said, "Be careful or you'll poke your eye out!" there was an actual possibility you might be playing with something that had the potential to do just that.

What yesterday's parents considered "playtime," today might be labeled "neglect." But perhaps we've swung a tad too far in the opposite direction. All of the warning labels, guardrails, safety nets and height requirements can make even the most rational parents, and kids, a bit paranoid. They make living sound downright hazardous. Which, of course, it is.

The human body is both remarkably resilient and incredible fragile. As parents, one of our greatest responsibilities, and deepest desires, is to keep our kids safe. Maybe that's one reason why video games are so popular. We allow our kids to control virtual characters who take risks we'd never allow our own children to take in real life.

Skateboarding, boxing, hockey, car racing... Our kids can do it all in the comfort and safety of our very own living rooms. They can go bowling, without the risk of a blister or infectious foot fungus from those fashion-forward bowling shoes available at a real alley. They can even read a book without ever touching a real page. Hence, no risk of paper cuts.

Real life always involves risk. Regardless of how conscientious we are, we can't protect our kids from everything. Broken bones—and broken hearts—are part of life. We can encourage them to use common sense and play it safe. Then all that's left to do is pray...and let them play.

Who ran to help me, when I fell,
And would some pretty story tell,
Or kiss the place to make it well?
My Mother.

Ann Taylor

Don't be too timid and squeamish...
All life is an experiment.
The more experiments you make,
the better.

Ralph Waldo Emerson

Prudence keeps life safe, but does
not often make it happy.

Samuel Johnson

*Only those who risk going too far
can possibly find out how far one
can go.*

    T. S. Eliot

*I long to put the experience of
fifty years at once into your young
lives, to give you at once the key of
that treasure chamber every gem
of which has cost me tears and struggles
and prayers, but you must work for
these inward treasures yourselves.*

    Harriet Beecher Stowe

*It is a happy talent to
know how to play.*

    Ralph Waldo Emerson

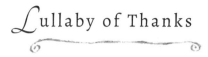Lullaby of Thanks

There are plenty of things to keep a mother up at night. A newborn's cry. Making certain your teen arrives home before curfew. Insomnia brought on by raging hormones. Constructing a jaunty eye patch for Pirate Day at school (which you learned about right before bedtime. Argghh...)

But when you can't sleep, don't anxiously count the minutes until the alarm goes off in the morning. Count your blessings, instead. Offer up a "thank you" to God for all of the gifts, big and small, you've received today. When you do, one of two things will happen. Either you'll pass the time sporting a smile and find yourself facing the new day feeling groggy, but grateful. Or you'll fall asleep before you can list them all. Either way, it's a more productive use of your time than counting imaginary sheep.

*The thankful heart will find,
in every hour, some heavenly blessings.*

    Henry Ward Beecher

*The best things are nearest:
breath in your nostrils,
light in your eyes,
flowers at your feet,
duties at your hand,
the path of God just before you.*

    Robert Louis Stevenson

*Reflect upon your present blessings,
of which every man has plenty;
not on your past misfortunes of
which all men have some.*

    Charles Dickens

An Endangered Species

Today, there's a species that teeters on the edge of extinction. Never before have sightings dipped this low. There are no activist groups or bumper stickers helping to rally the cry that something precious and irreplaceable is disappearing from our homes and our schools. What's worse, mothers are mainly to blame.

Yes, in days gone by, average children could be seen everywhere. Almost every family had at least one. But according to Christmas letters, social media and coffee break chatter, the only children that remain are exceptional. Each one is a musical prodigy, future pro-football quarterback or potential hand model. Classes for gifted children are so common that soon gifted children will become, well...the new average. Somewhere, there's a whole underground network of average children whose parents have hidden them away. Perhaps their families were shamed into no longer sending Christmas letters, afraid to announce publicly that little Johnny shows little aptitude, or interest, in anything other than burping the alphabet. If this average child happens to have siblings—exceptional siblings—the family may send out a multi-paged holiday missive to herald their many accomplishments. But little Johnny will be reduced to a single sentence: "As for John, he continues to keep us on our toes."

Together, we can save little Johnny—and all of the other average children just like him. We can help them stand tall, proud to be exactly who they were created to be. No more, no less. Average kids aren't losers. Neither are those who've been labeled "below average." Every individual is a precious, irreplaceable, uniquely gifted creation. Our intrinsic worth is found in who we are, not in what we can or can't do.

As moms, if we can understand and accept this truth about ourselves, we'll naturally pass it on to our kids...along with the fact that in our eyes, our children will always be exceptional, regardless of how average they may be.

*In the eyes of its mother every
beetle is a gazelle.*

    Proverb

*My child is a Phenomenon,
really the most wonderful Natural
Production I ever beheld.*

    Elizabeth Lady Webster

*When I approach a child he inspires
in me two sentiments: tenderness
for what he is, and respect for what
he may become.*

    Louis Pasteur

*A show-off is any child more
talented than your own.*

    Saying

*Every human being is intended
to have a character of his own;
to be what no others are, and to do
what no other can do.*

    William Ellery Channing

*Use what talents you possess;
the woods would be very silent
if no birds sang there except
those that sang best.*

    Henry Van Dyke

The Oh-So-Great Outdoors

Moms used to be referred to as "homemakers." What a lovely description of what we work so hard to do! We strive to make where we live feel inviting, safe and comfy. Our goal is for our family, as well as anyone who crosses our threshold, to feel "at home." But, the more comfortable home is, the less we may care to leave. With cable TV, the internet and pizza delivery, we could be tempted to spend all our free time relaxing within the confines of our humble abode.

But there's so much more to the world. God's creation is filled with beauty, wonder and mystery. Exploring it is not only good for our bodies, but good for our relationships and our souls. Nurture a hunger for outdoor adventure in your kids. Hike mountain trails together. Gather seashells along the shore. Camp near secluded lakes. God's given us the whole world to call home. Let's enjoy every corner we can.

*It is perhaps a more fortunate
destiny to have a taste for collecting
shells than to be born a millionaire.*

    Robert Louis Stevenson

*Earth's crammed with heaven.
And every common bush afire
with God.*

    Elizabeth Barrett Browning

*You will never find your bliss
if you prefer comfort.*

When I give, I give myself.
    Walt Whitman

One mark of a good mom is that her children run into her arms, even when her hands are empty.

A child, like your stomach, doesn't need all you can afford to give it.
    Frank A. Clark

The Gift That Fits Just Right

It's tempting to express our love for our kids with our credit cards. After all, getting new stuff makes them happy. And giving them gifts is fun for us, too! But lavishing our children with goodies isn't a win-win situation. It can lead them to believe that new stuff is a necessity, that what they want equals what they need.

Another temptation is that we can rely on giving gifts as our shortcut to building a relationship. When we're busy, we've blown it or we feel as though we're not connecting as well as we should, it's easy to give a gift and feel as though the problem is fixed.

Giving ourselves—our time, our attention and our hearts—can cost us more than an expensive gift. But it's worth it. That kind of gift won't break or go out of style. It can't be lost or stolen. It's a gift that fills our children's hearts, instead of their closets.

Fan Fare

For a mom, there's something more painful than childbirth. It's seeing your kids fail. Maybe they don't get the job they've been hanging their future on or the part they'd hoped for in the school play. It could be something as small as failing to fully cook their first Thanksgiving turkey or as big as ending their marriage. Regardless of what it is, when they hurt, we hurt.

But their lives are not ours. They have the freedom to make their own choices. Sometimes, we may believe those choices hinder them from reaching the amazing potential we see so clearly in them. Frankly, at times like these it's hard for us to keep our mouths shut. But we try. As for the other times, when disappointment or heartbreak seem to come out of nowhere, we just want to make certain our kids know we're rooting for them—and that rain or shine, we'll remain their biggest fans.

You cannot teach a child to take care of himself unless you will let him take care of himself. He will make mistakes, and out of these mistakes will come his wisdom.

Henry Ward Beecher

Love me when I least deserve it, because that's when I really need it.

Proverb

Success is going from failure to failure without loss of enthusiasm.

Sir Winston Churchill

*A mother is the truest friend we have, when
trials heavy and sudden, fall upon us;
when adversity takes the place of prosperity;
when friends who rejoice with us
in our sunshine desert us; when trouble
thickens around us, still will she cling to us,
and endeavor by her kind precepts and
counsels to dissipate the clouds of darkness,
and cause peace to return to our hearts.*

Washington Irving

*No distance of place or lapse of time
can lessen the friendship of those who
are thoroughly persuaded of each
other's worth.*

Robert Southey

*Secret to a happy life: Treat your friends
like family and your family like friends!*

The Best of Friends

Friendship between moms and their adult children is an amazing gift. It's also a tricky one. After all, we all know way too much about each other. We've seen each other at our best and at our worst. We feel so comfortable in one another's company that we're liable to say anything at any time—often before thinking it through. If we're not careful, we may find ourselves taking each other for granted in ways we would never dream of doing with the other people in our circle of friends.

With so many shared memories, we may feel as though we know each other inside and out. But there's always more to discover about those we love. Let's explore! Ask questions. Really listen. Expect the unexpected! Most of all, let's treat one another with the same courtesy, respect, commitment and candor as we do our dearest friends. After all, moms and their children are more than just chance acquaintances. We're linked by love for a lifetime.

How Do You Spell MOM?

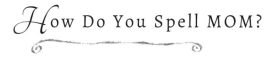

It's been said, "Mother is another word for love." However, some lesser-quoted synonyms include (but are certainly not limited to!):

Loan officer
Historian
Fashion consultant
Cheerleader
Dressing room valet
On-call babysitter
911 operator
Therapist
Home health care consultant
Legal counsel
 and FRIEND!

They talk about a woman's sphere as though it had a limit;
There's not a place in Earth or Heaven,
There's not a task to mankind given,
There's not a blessing or a woe,
There's not a whispered yes or no,
There's not a life, or death, or birth,
That has a feather's weight of worth—
Without a woman in it.

    Kate Field

Being There

What do you think your kids want most from you? Well…YOU! They want you to be around to love them, to dote on them, to brag about them and, when the time comes, to help them parent their own children. One way you can help fill this desire of theirs is by taking care of yourself physically, mentally, emotionally and spiritually.

Exercise. Eat a balanced diet. Get enough sleep. Ask for help when you need it. Spend time with a supportive circle of friends. Pray. You know what you need to do. The tricky part is doing it. Moms are famous for putting everyone else's needs before their own. That may look like self-less sacrifice, but it can actually be self-destructive. And it can even be self-centered—driven by the need to be needed.

Care for your family by caring for your own needs, as well as theirs. It's just one more way to love them well.

*Those who think they have not time
for bodily exercise will sooner or later
have to find time for illness.*

    Edward Stanley

*Health is like money, we never
have a true idea of its value until
we lose it.*

    Josh Billings

*It is thy duty oftentimes to do what
thou wouldst not; thy duty, too,
to leave undone that thou wouldst do.*

    Thomas à Kempis

The Job of a Lifetime

This job called "motherhood" is a whirlwind of activity, emotion and stretch marks. There are no prerequisites, no official training and no quitting time. There's also no job description, because every mother's would read differently and take a lifetime to write. As for job performance, it can't be measured by conventional means. That's because we've been entrusted with the care of a highly volatile and extremely fragile substance—one that can exercise free will. It's like being responsible for plutonium with legs and an attitude. Not to mention hormones. Talk about a challenge.

Compensation is equally difficult to gauge. It may be years before we receive the full benefits of our efforts. Even then, it's only in retrospect that we become aware of what those truly are. But, let's face it…from the very first moment we see our child's face, we know there's no other job we'd rather have.

Perhaps the greatest social service that can be rendered by anybody to the country and to mankind is to bring up a family. But here again, because there is nothing to sell, there is a very general disposition to regard a married woman's work as no work at all, and to take it as a matter of course that she should not be paid for it.

George Bernard Shaw

Men make a camp; a swarm of bees a comb; Birds make a nest; a woman makes a home.

Arthur Guiterman

Making the decision to have a child— it's momentous. It is to decide forever to have your heart go walking around outside your body.

Elizabeth Stone

Against the Grain

There will be days when we feel our kids rub us the wrong way. When they get on our nerves and test our patience. Days when they're unreasonable or irresponsible, when they whine and complain, provoke their siblings or break our favorite doodad.

Instead of viewing these days as the "trials" of motherhood, let's consider them as our own self-help workshop. When our kids go against the grain is when they become the sandpaper we need to smooth out the rough edges of our own character. Godly traits such as patience, forgiveness, self-sacrifice, generosity and unconditional love don't develop as we sit and watch TV. They're honed under fire in our daily lives, most often in our own homes. Our children truly are gifts from God, in countless unexpected ways.

*God sends us children for another purpose
than merely to keep up the race—to enlarge
our hearts; to make us unselfish and full of
kindly sympathies and affections; to give our
souls higher aims; to call out our faculties;
to extended enterprise and exertion; and to
bring round our firesides bright faces and
happy smiles, and loving, tender hearts.
My soul blesses the great Father every
day that He has gladdened the earth
with little children.*

    Mary Howitt

*That energy which makes a child
hard to manage is what afterward
makes him a manager of life.*

    Henry Ward Beecher

*Children need love, especially when
they do not deserve it.*

    Harold Hulbert

Out in the Open

Expectations are sneaky little things. They seem innocent enough. But they can get buried in our subconscious and blow up in the face of someone we love. Including our kids. Hoping and dreaming are one thing. But when we expect something, we run the risk of disappointment, and resentment, if it doesn't happen.

What expectations do you have of your children? Really…How about when it comes to keeping their rooms clean? The grades they receive? The profession they choose to pursue? The spouse they choose to marry? How often they'll call once they leave home? How they'll celebrate Mother's Day?

Expectations don't have to be destructive. They simply need to be realistic, verbalized and agreed upon. Once they're out in the open, they're much easier to control—and dismantle if need be.

Life is so constructed that the event does not, cannot, will not, match the expectation.

    Charlotte Brontë

A child's soul is more tender and vulnerable than the finest or tenderest plant, and a cross look or a rough touch or an unkind tone is often sufficient to inflict a savage blow. God grant that every mother may recognize in time the sacredness and tenderness of the soul of her child!

    Hannah Whitall Smith

Make it your habit to not be critical about small things.

    Edward Everett Hale

Special Delivery

There's a gift you can give your kids that costs you nothing more than a few minutes of your time. It's one they'll never outgrow. They'll never suffer from having too much of it, even if you provide it daily. They may be unaware they're receiving it, but that doesn't mean it won't make a positive difference in their lives. And it doesn't matter if they are in the same room or on the other side of the world; it will always arrive just when they need it most. That gift is prayer.

Prayer is a gift of love, both to God and to your children. It may be hard to believe, but He loves them even more than you do. So, wrap up your hopes, dreams, care and concern in a prayer. Then, send it on it's way. Today.

A mother's prayers, silent and gentle, can never miss the road to the throne of all bounty.

    Henry Ward Beecher

I remember my mother's prayers and they have always followed me. They have clung to me all my life.

    Abraham Lincoln

God bless mother and daddy, my brother and sister, and save the king. And, oh God, do take care of yourself, because if anything happens to you, we're all sunk.

    Adlai E. Stevenson
    (quoting a child's prayer in a speech)

The Truth About Mother's Day

Imagine a day where you're waited on hand and foot. Family and friends lavish you with gifts, flowers and affection. Total strangers voice their best wishes. All the little things you do, the ones that go unnoticed the other 364 days of the year, are praised from the pulpit of churches around the country. Top that off with a sumptuous buffet; one you didn't cook and won't have to clean up. The only thing required of you is to enjoy yourself from the moment you awake until an early bedtime.

Yeah, that's what others think Mother's Day is like.

We know differently.

Mother's Day is really about your cancelling all of your plans when you hear those fateful words, "Mommy, I don't feel good." It's about having kids eat the entire box of chocolates your husband gave you just this morning while you're getting ready for church. It's about cleaning up the mess after being served breakfast in bed.

Yes, it's all those things, but most of all it's about discovering how deeply you can love someone, sight unseen. Someone you've had the privilege of giving birth to or adopting as your own. Someone who calls you "Mom." That's what Mother's Day is all about.

As for Father's Day? Well, it looks like Mother's Day did in our heads. That's because mothers plan it, execute it and clean up after it. Kids just deliver the Father's Day card Mom bought and the breakfast-in-bed Mom made, yet kids get all the credit. And if the kids get a fever on Father's Day, Mom holds their hair back while they get sick.

Mother's Day may not be all it's cracked up to be. But being a mother is. Our kids are the best gift we could ever receive, any day of the year.

*Truly there is nothing in the
world so blessed or so sweet as
the heritage of children.*

Margaret Oliphant

*A man's work is from sun to sun,
But a mother's work is never done.*

Author Unkown

*What would men be without women?
Scarce, sir, mighty scarce.*

Mark Twain

In conversation father can
Do many wondrous things;
He's built upon a wiser plan
Than presidents or kings.
He knows the ins and outs of each
And every deep transaction;
We look to him for theories,
But look to ma for action.

    Edgar A. Guest

Be a "Pass It On" Mom

Motherhood provides on-the-job training. The irony seems to be that once your kids are finally ready to head out on their own, you've just about got the hang of raising them. So what do you do with all those years of hard-earned experience? Help your kids when they become parents? Certainly. (At least to the extent they ask for your help!)

But there's another audience that could really use what you have to offer: a generation of new moms asking the same questions you did when you were in their shoes. Why not expand your circle of friends to include a few new moms? Don't wait for them to seek out your help. Treat them to coffee. Offer to babysit. Bring over dinner one evening, so they don't have to cook. Don't push yourself on them. Just be the kind of friend you longed for when you had young kids. Put what you've learned to good use—and receive a friend in return. Now, there's a timeless two-for-one deal!

*If you have knowledge,
let others light their candles at it.*

    Margaret Fuller

*Give what you have. To someone
it may be better than you dare
to think.*

    Henry Wadsworth Longfellow

*Life can only be understood backwards;
but it must be lived forwards.*

    Søren Kierkegaard

*Life is a country that the old have
seen, and lived in. Those who have
to travel through it can only learn
the way from them.*

    Joseph Joubert

The manner of giving is worth more than the gift.

Pierre Corneille

Every artist was first an amateur.

Ralph Waldo Emerson

A child's attitude toward everything is an artist's attitude.

Willa Cather

It took me four years to paint like Raphael, but a lifetime to paint like a child.

Pablo Picasso

Handmade with Love

Moms receive so many lovely gifts from their children. Reams of paper covered with indecipherable scribbles. Clay pots shaped like amoebas. Cards made out of toilet paper. Three-foot plastic lanyards woven at summer camp. Spray-painted gold brooches made from dried macaroni…

The question is, where to house so many priceless treasures? Throwing them away isn't an option. The kids always find out (and their future therapist will hear all about your treachery). So, unless you live in a house the size of the Smithsonian, the only reasonable choice is re-gifting. Yes, when your children have grown to adulthood (and have attics, basements and storage units of their own), give them what they really want for Christmas: a blast from their very own past. Just beware of what your grandkids may have gift-wrapped specially for you.

The Wow Factor

As any mother knows, kids have the power to turn our world upside-down, regardless of their age! But if you turn MOM upside-down, what do you get? WOW! Coincidence? Perhaps. But somehow, when life is at its most challenging and chaotic, that's when moms tend to shine. Under pressure our priorities rise to the surface. And like a pot roast in a pressure cooker, moms seem to come out of those demanding, life-changing times even more tender than before.

Love will do that to you. When the well-being of our children is on the line, our energy, strength and creativity go on high alert. We find we can, and will, do things we never thought we could. So, don't downplay the "wow factor" of you. In big and small ways, you really are amazing.

When God thought of Mother,
He must have laughed with satisfaction
...so rich, so deep, so divine,
so full of soul, power and beauty
was the conception!

    Henry Ward Beecher

Nobody has ever measured,
not even poets, how much the
heart can hold.

    Zelda Fitzgerald

A mother is one to whom you
hurry when you are troubled.

    Emily Dickinson

Everybody knows that a good mother gives her children a feeling of trust and stability. She is their earth. She is the one they can count on for the things that matter most of all. She is their food and their bed and the extra blanket when it grows cold in the night; she is their warmth and their health and their shelter; she is the one they want to be near when they cry. She is the only person in the whole world in a whole lifetime who can be these things to her children. There is no substitute for her. Somehow even her clothes feel different to her children's hands from anybody else's clothes. Only to touch her skirt or her sleeve makes a troubled child feel better.

Katherine Butler Hathaway

*There's no vocabulary
For love within a family,
love that's lived in
But not looked at,
love within the light of which
All else is seen,
the love within which
All other love finds speech.
This love is silent.*

     T. S. Eliot

Finding Your Funny Bone

Every mom can use a little more giggle in her git-along. So, why not be proactive about adding laughter to your life? A good belly laugh reduces stress hormones and amps up our immune system. Our bodies also view laughter as a form of exercise! What sounds like more fun: watching a funny movie with friends or getting all sweaty at the gym?

What's more, every kid knows that a mom with a sense of humor doesn't get angry as often as a mom who lacks one. Seeing the irony or silliness in a situation can relieve a lot of tension and turn a would-be disaster into a much-heralded family memory. To keep your sense of humor in shape, give your funny bone a workout. Seek out funny movies and books. Hang out with people who make you laugh. Choose to look for the humor hiding in every day situations. Then don't hold back—let go and laugh.

*The most wasted day of all is
that on which we have not laughed.*

    Nicolas Chamfort

*Humor is the great thing,
the saving thing. The minute
it crops up, all our irritations
and resentments slip away
and a sunny spirit takes
their place.*

    Mark Twain

*We cannot really love anybody
with whom we never laugh.*

    Agnes Repplier

*To every thing there is a season,
and a time to every purpose under the
heaven...a time to weep, and a time
to laugh; a time to mourn, and a
time to dance.*

    Ecclesiastes 3:1,4

A Workout for Your Funny Bone

A young mother was pushing a stroller carrying her twin sons through the parking lot of a department store. An elderly woman walked up to her, took a peek inside at the babies, who were dressed in matching blue outfits, and then said with great affection, "How precious! And both boys...What do you want your next child to be?"

The new mom replied, "A grandchild!"

Did you hear about the kids dressed as cowboys who wore paper pants, paper shirts, paper boots and paper hats?

The sheriff arrested them for rustling.

The minute little Janey got home from school she excitedly told her mother, "Today in class we learned how to make babies!"

Trying to keep her cool, her mother responded, "That's interesting, honey. How do you do that?"

Janey said confidently, "Change the 'y' to 'i' and add 'es.'"

An elementary teacher was preparing to discuss magnetism with her class. She held a magnet over a box filled with pins and then said, "My name begins with *m* and I pick up things. What am I?"

A girl in the front row immediately yelled out, "MOM!"

So, You Have a Daughter...

Having a daughter is like giving birth to a future best friend. What an incredible gift! But you never know who you're going to meet. Your daughter may grow to be like you in so many ways that her friends think it's kind of scary. Or you two may be so different that you wonder if the hospital accidentally switched babies at birth. Regardless of who your daughter grows up to be, you both have a lot of loving and learning to do.

Help her bloom. Listen to her. Learn from her. Look for the very best in her. Do what you can to help her become the amazing woman God created her to be. Then (and this is the really tough part) give her a little push out of the nest when the time is right. Give her room to grow and permission to go. True love not only can handle it, but encourage it and grow exponentially stronger through it.

The amicable loosening of the bond between daughter and mother is one of the most difficult tasks of education.

Alice Balint

A daughter is a treasure— and a cause of sleeplessness.

Ben Sirach

And thou shalt in thy daughter see, This picture, once, resembled thee.

Ambrose Philips

A perplexing and ticklish possession is a daughter.

Thomas Hardy

So, You Have a Son…

Raising a daughter feels a bit like raising yourself, while raising a son can feel like you're venturing into foreign territory. After all, you have the basic materials for a man in your midst! So, take advantage of the opportunity. Do your future daughter-in-law a favor by helping your son mature into a man who can take care of himself.

Go ahead. Love your son. Delight in him. Praise him. But, also teach him how to pick up after himself, follow through on a commitment and treat the women in his life with tenderness and respect. Help him be the kind of guy every other mother will want for a son-in-law! At the same time, you'll find yourself raising a son you'll proudly brag about for years to come.

Sons are the anchors of a mother's life.

Sophocles

*Don't wait to make your son a
great man. Make him a great boy.*

Author Unknown

*Let France have good mothers,
and she will have good sons.*

Napoleon Bonaparte

*Happy is the son whose faith in
his mother remains unchallenged.*

Louisa May Alcott

Let's Get Real to the "Before Children" Era

Think back...way back to the "Before Children" era. What kind of mother did you picture you'd be? Many of us imagined ourselves as the cool moms. Our daughters would beg to borrow our clothing. Our teenage sons would plead with us to play drums for their rock band. We'd all get matching friendship bracelets. We'd have the wisdom of Solomon, the patience of Job and the fashion sense of Jackie O.

Where did we develop a picture like this? Blame it on reruns of black and white sitcoms. Back then, TV moms wore pearls in the kitchen. They could get the truth out of their kids with just the raise of an eyebrow. They resolved every crisis in under 30 minutes—and never forgot to take the homemade cookies out of the oven before they were reduced to ash.

Fast forward to reality. Unlike those early sitcoms, the real world is anything but black and white. There are no easy answers or simple fixes when it comes to parenting. We may never be as calm, cool and collected as those TV moms. But that's okay. They never had the opportunity to live in the real world. Let's face it: we get the better deal.

So, let's hold tightly to reality. Even when it isn't perfect. Sure, being the cool mom would be nice. But so would wearing size 0 skinny jeans or being able to belt out a tune like a diva rock star. Some things just aren't gonna happen. We may not be cool, but we are committed. As moms, we may not always know best, but we're also not ashamed to pray, ask for advice, apologize or call for a "time out."

And when our kids look back on their childhood, if they don't describe us as really perfect, fashion forward or cool, that's okay. What matters most is they know we were "real."

*You will find, as you look back
upon your life, that the moments
when you have really lived are the
moments when you have done
things in the spirit of love.*

Henry Drummond

*The best things you can give your
children, next to good habits,
are good memories.*

Sydney J. Harris

*The happiness of life is made up
of minute fractions—the little,
soon-forgotten charities of a kiss
or smile, a kind look or heartfelt
compliment.*

Samuel Taylor Coleridge

*Most mothers are
instinctive philosophers.*

    Harriet Beecher Stowe

*Example is not the main
thing in influencing others.
It is the only thing.*

    Albert Schweitzer

*Perhaps a better woman,
after all,
With chubby children
hanging on my neck
To keep me low and wise.*

    Elizabeth Barrett Browning

A Little Peace and Quiet

Are you a mom on the edge? You may have been there so long that you don't recognize how tightly your fingers are trying to hold onto your sanity. We've all been there. But the real question is: how do we get back? How do we regain balance in our lives, even if our family's circumstances are set on full-tilt?

There's no magic cure or quick fix. But moment-by-moment we can make tiny adjustments in our perspective that will eventually realign our habits and our hearts with a more positive and peaceful state of mind.

First, you need to find a quiet spot. Even five minutes locked in your bathroom will do. Close your eyes. Picture yourself in God's arms. Simply say the word, "Help." Then, just breathe. Just be fully present, with your cares locked outside the door.

Don't get too excited. They'll be waiting for you when you come out. But you won't come out the same mom you were when you went in.

We all need time to just "be" in our lives. Time to be quiet, inside and out. Time to listen for God's still, small voice amidst the clamor of the chaos around us. It's been said that, "We're human be-ings, not human do-ings." But "doing" feels like we're accomplishing something. "Being" feels lazy and self-indulgent, like a waste of our time. But sometimes that's exactly what we need, a genuine time-out.

We force our kids to take one when they lose control. Perhaps we need to get in the habit of doing the same for ourselves. Even if we appear calm, cool and collected on the surface, if we're falling apart on the inside it's time to stop—just breathe and be.

*How rare to find a soul still
enough to hear God speak.*

François Fénelon

*Drop Thy still dews of quietness
Till all our strivings cease;
Take from our souls the strain and stress,
And let our ordered lives confess
The beauty of Thy peace.*

John Greenleaf Whittier

*In quiet places,
reason abounds.*

Adlai Stevenson

God hath not promised skies always blue,
Flower-strewn pathways all our lives through;
God hath not promised sun without rain,
Joy without sorrow, peace without pain.

But God hath promised strength for the day,
Rest for the labor, light for the way,
Grace for the trials, help from above,
Unfailing sympathy, undying love.

      Annie Johnson Flint

Through a Mother's Eyes

A mother's eyes are her children's most favorable mirror. That's because when we look at our kids, we see more than who they are today. We see their potential. We're not blind to their weaknesses. We simply know that isn't the most important thing about them. We choose to focus on their strengths. We see what's beautiful, interesting, worth knowing and worth nurturing in them.

That's why one of our deepest desires is that the world would see our children the way we do. We're not naïve. We're fully aware they'll be judged by first impressions, by their appearance, by pre-conceived notions others may hold. That's why we lavish our children with love, encouragement and prayer, so they'll be able to hold their heads high, even when the world can't quite see just how remarkable they truly are.

*Mothers see the angel in us
because the angel is there.*

Booth Tarkington

*Sweet is the smile of home;
the mutual look
When hearts are
of each other sure.*

John Keble

*The supreme happiness of life
is the conviction of being loved
for yourself, or, more correctly,
being loved in spite of yourself.*

Victor Hugo

*There is more to life than
increasing its speed.*

    Mahatma Gandhi

*On every level of life from
housework to heights of prayer,
in all judgment and efforts
to get things done, hurry and
impatience are sure marks of
the amateur.*

    Evelyn Underhill

*Life is short and we never have
enough time for gladdening
the hearts of those who travel the
way with us. Oh, be swift to love!
Make haste to be kind.*

    Henri Frédéric Amiel

The Pace of the Human Race

The older we get, the more quickly the years seem to fly by. So, we try to stuff as much "life" as we can into every day. But the more activities and appointments we cram into our family's schedule, the less we seem to enjoy.

Just because we're part of the human race, doesn't mean we have to run as fast as we can everywhere we go. We set the pace of our lives. And our children learn to mimic that pace. When we make a conscious effort to underschedule our lives a bit, we allow for breathing room in our day. That leaves us time to watch the sunset. Time to talk with those we love. Time for the unexpected. Time to laugh…or cry. Time to enjoy the little blessings tucked away in the quiet corners of today.

Just Because We Share DNA...

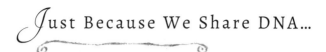

As mothers, we share so much with our children. However, once they're on the brink of adulthood, we need to make it perfectly clear that just because we're related, it does not mean we're obligated to share absolutely everything. This includes:
 our cars,
 our PIN numbers,
 our laundry services,
 our computer passwords,
 the same taste in movies and music,
 the entire contents of our fridge
  OR our dessert!

Maternal Workout

I bend over backwards for my kids,
Stretch our budget and push my luck.
I even jump to conclusions,
When my hormones run amok.
I work hard to lift my kids' spirits
And I try to pull my weight.
So don't ask me if I exercise;
My current workout's great!

Vicki J. Kuyper

Exceptions to the Rule

It begins with bedtime stories. We encourage our children to dream, to imagine, to wish upon a star. We help open their little minds to possibility, mystery and asking questions. As they mature, we focus more on rule keeping...bed times, bath times, chores, good grades and good grooming.

Along the way, let's not forget that sometimes it's okay to break the rules. (That applies to us, as well as our children.) To wear socks that don't match, just because we think it's fun. To stay up past bedtime. To eat breakfast for dinner. To watch the sunrise, instead of making our bed. To take a chance. To dream big. To not go along with the crowd. To remember there are exceptions to every rule. And sometimes, that exception just may be us.

*The home is not the one tame
place in the world of adventure.
It is the one wild place in the
world of rules and set tasks.*

    G. K. Chesterton

*The young man knows the rules,
but the old man knows the exceptions.*

Oliver Wendell Holmes

*I still live in and on the sunshine
of my childhood.*

Christian Morgenstern

*Oh, the love of a mother,
love which none can forget.*

Victor Hugo

*My mother had a slender,
small body, but a large heart—
a heart so large that everybody's
griefs and joys found welcome in it,
and hospitable accommodation.*

Mark Twain

*Motherhood:
All love begins and ends there.*

Robert Browning

Mom's Secret Recipe

Moms spend a lot of time in the kitchen. When we're not cooking or cleaning, we're putting away groceries in preparation for another week of cooking and cleaning. But have you ever stopped to think about how moms are like a wholesome meal?

We nourish our children physically, mentally, emotionally and spiritually. We strengthen them with our words and prayers. We add a little spice to their day in unexpected ways. When they're feeling empty, we fill them up with kindness and encouragement. We sweeten their lives with kisses and cuddles. And tomorrow, when they're hungry once more, we do it all over again.

There is an angel in the family,
who, with a mysterious influence of charm,
sweetness and love,
makes the accomplishment of duties
less arduous, pains less bitter.
The angel of the family is the woman.
Mother, Wife, Sister.
Woman is the caress of life,
the gentleness of love.

        Giuseppe Mazzini

The mother memories that are closest to my heart are the small gentle ones that I have carried over from the days of my childhood. They are not profound, but they have stayed with me through life, and when I am very old, they will still be near...Memories of mother drying my tears, reading aloud, cutting cookies and singing as she did, listening to prayers I said as I knelt with my forehead pressed against her knee, tucking me in bed and turning down the light. They have carried me through the years and given my life such a firm foundation that it does not rock beneath flood or tempest.

      Margaret Sanger

Oooops...

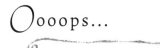

No matter how much we love our kids, there will be days when we blow it. We'll lose our temper. We'll say words we wish we could take back. We'll be inattentive and not listen to what our kids have to say. We'll treat our children like an inconvenience, instead of a blessing. We'll be less than the mom we long to be.

There is no perfect mom. Or child. That's why true forgiveness is a part of true love. It's a gift we need to extend to ourselves, as well as those around us. Forgiveness isn't simply letting ourselves off the hook. It's feeling the weight of what we've done, doing what's in our power to fix what we can, recommitting ourselves to do better in the future—and then leaving that regret in the past so we can move forward. In the same way that we wouldn't punish our kids over and over for a past offense, we need to deal with what we've done. Once. Learn from it. Then, move on.

*Have patience with all things,
but chiefly have patience with
yourself. Do not lose courage in
considering your own imperfections,
but instantly set about remedying them—
every day begin the task anew.*

    Francis de Sales

*Forgiveness is the answer to the
child's dream of a miracle by which
what is broken is made whole again,
what is soiled is again made clean.*

    Dag Hammarskjöld

*Failure is God's own tool for carving
some of the finest outlines in the
character of his children.*

    Thomas Hodgkin

Home Builders

Picture yourself as a lone carpenter, building your home. It would be quite the project! You'd not only have to build the frame, you'd have to pour the foundation, install the wiring, put on the roof...you get the idea. Now, imagine if you had two or three or four others helping you. How much more efficient, and fun, would the project be?

It's tempting to do everything ourselves. After all, we feel as though we'll do it right. But, moms need to be Team Builders, instead of Lone Rangers. We need to enlist our kids' help around the house. They need the experience and we could use the extra helping hands. Even as adults, when our kids come over for dinner, it's okay to ask them to bring something—and then help with the dishes afterwards. Wherever and whenever families gather is home. It's being built one memory at a time, with everyone pitching in.

A mother is not a person to lean on but a person to make leaning unnecessary.

　　　　Dorothy Canfield Fisher

It is impossible to estimate too highly the value and the helpfulness of a true home of love. Home is a shelter. Young lives nest there and find warmth and protection.

　　　　J. R. Miller

*A house is built of logs and stone,
Of tiles and posts and piers;
A home is built of loving deeds
That stand a thousand years.*

　　　　Victor Hugo

Teens...A Cautionary Tale

It's a good thing God designed us to begin life as babies. If moms gave birth to teens, every child would be an only child. Teens can be moody, self-centered and demanding. Kind of like babies—only with acne and attitudes. Not to mention a driver's license. Logic and rational thought may be foreign concepts to the adolescent psyche. But don't despair. If you are currently raising teens, consider them a cautionary tale. As they are so you shall be. That's because we lucky moms have a second adolescence in our future. It's called menopause.

When "the change" arrives, rational thought once again goes out the window. Our mind short-circuits as we're driven crazy by hormones (or a lack thereof). Our complexion breaks out (with acne *and* age spots!). Our bodies change shape (only instead of a getting cute and curvy, we tend toward round and lumpy). And we stress about the future. *Who will I be and what will I do when the kids leave the nest? And what if they come BACK???*

So don't fear the teen years. Those kids will grow up and be making fun of you before you know it.

*Human life is a continuous thread
which each of us spins to his own
pattern, rich and complex in meaning.
There are no natural knots in it.
Yet knots form, almost always
in adolescence.*

> Henri Estienne

*Common sense is the collection
of prejudices aquired by the age
of eighteen.*

> Albert Einstein

*When I was a boy of fourteen, my father
was so ignorant I could hardly stand to
have the old man around. But when I got
to be twenty-one, I was astonished at how
much he had learned in seven years.*

> Mark Twain

Adolescence: When your kids stop asking where they came from and start refusing to tell you where they're going.

Vicki J. Kuyper

Children grow up so quickly and leave us, and I would long that mine should take nothing, but the recollection of love and happiness from their home with them into the world's fight, knowing that they have here always a safe harbor and open arms to comfort and encourage them when they are in trouble.

Grand Duchess Princess Alice Maud Mary, daughter of Queen Victoria

Train up a child in the way he should go: and when he is old, he will not depart from it.

Proverbs 22:6

Kids = Fountain of Youth

Having children on the brink of adulthood keeps a mother young. After all, it's you who tell us our jeans are too high and our driving is too slow. You help update our slang, our shoes and our tastebuds. Who knew we should be eating cake pops instead of cupcakes, beignets instead of doughnuts and kale chips instead of French fries? You've opened our eyes to gluten-free, vegan, organic and dining at food trucks. Where would we be without you?

Yes, without you we'd continue to hum in the grocery store, convinced they've improved their musical selection—when the truth is the sound track of our generation has been demoted to elevator music. Thank goodness you've introduced us to contemporary stations, with words we can't understand and a beat we can't dance to. Thanks to you we no longer look or act old. We're simply more aware of how old we really are.

*When grace is joined with wrinkles,
it is adorable.*

Victor Hugo

*Life would be infinitely happier if we
could only be born at the age of eighty
and gradually approach eighteen.*

Mark Twain

*It's not that age brings childhood back again,
Age merely shows what children we remain.*

Johann Wolfgang von Goethe

But We Always Do It This Way...

When you were a kid, you may have received new pajamas every Christmas Eve, always grilled hot dogs on the Fourth of July and dyed eggs the night before Easter year-after-year. Family traditions can be a source of cherished memories. But they can also feel like an obligation that can't be broken.

As moms, we usually start and maintain family traditions. What a creative privilege! But, if we find ourselves dreading a tradition, instead of looking forward to it, let's rethink the "always" part. We can skip a year, or scale it down, during bumpy seasons of our lives. We can even nix a tradition or replace it with something altogether new. Yes, we have the parental power! If there's pressure from extended family to keep a tradition going, let's show our kids how to blaze a new path while still showing respect for those with a different point of view. Let's start a tradition of honesty and simplicity!

All of our life is a celebration for us.

Clement of Alexandria

Tradition is a guide and not a jailer.

W. Somerset Maugham

Tradition, which is always old,
is at the same time ever new because
it is always reviving—born again
in each new generation, to be lived
and applied in a new and particular way.

Thomas Merton

Open Letter to Grown Children Everywhere

Dear Kids, please take note: We don't want to push you. (Well, maybe just a nudge...) But we'd really appreciate it if you'd get married. It's not that we're desperate for grandkids. (Okay, so, maybe we are...)

But, what we REALLY want is a chance to dress up. An opportunity like that presents itself so rarely these days. But your wedding (and shower and rehearsal dinner) would give us the chance to shop for something lovely and flouncy. Something that would make us feel young and beautiful. Even if just for a few hours.

Of course, we do want you to be happy. So, take your time and get engaged to an absolutely, fantastic person who loves you more than life itself. But keep that engagement short. Think of your mother!
P.S. And whatever you do, don't elope!

*As long as a woman can look
ten years younger than her daughter
she is perfectly satisfied.*

Oscar Wilde

*Whatever you do, put romance
and enthusiasm into the life
of your children.*

Margaret Ramsey MacDonald

*When your child's wedding day arrives
There's something you should know:
It's the height of multi-tasking—
Both holding on and letting go.*

Vicki J. Kuyper

Be a Bridge Builder

Your kids will never be able to walk in your shoes. Sure, they may become parents, but they will never know what it was like to be *their* parent. And you—even though you are an amazing mother who knows your children better than almost anyone else on earth—will never really know what it's like to see the world through their eyes.

The parent/child relationship can get tricky at times because we're so close that we forget we can be so different. On occasion, that can cause a rift in our relationship. If this happens, it's time to put our pride, and our differences, aside and build a bridge of reconciliation. Yes, it takes two to mend a relational rift. But it only takes one to make the first move.

He who forgives ends the quarrel.

Proverb

We like someone because.
We love someone although.

Henrí de Montherlant

He who cannot forgive breaks
the bridge over which he himself
must pass.

George Herbert

*Be kind, for everyone you meet
is fighting a hard battle.*

Philo

*Home is not where you live
but where they understand you.*

Christian Morgenstern

*Mighty is the force of motherhood!
It transforms all things by its vital heat.*

George Eliot

Mothering Others

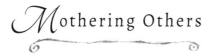

Not every child is fortunate enough to have a mom like you. But that doesn't mean they can't be nurtured by a mother's love... namely, yours.

There will be opportunities throughout your life—and your own seasons of motherhood—when you will become aware of someone in need. That "someone" may be a friend of your kids, a child in your neighborhood or community, or a grown woman who could use the support and encouragement of an "older woman" in her life. Open your heart wide enough to invite them in. Lavish a little love on them without expecting anything in return. Through friendship (or even foster parenting) you can provide a sense of family to someone who may feel all alone in the world. After all, in a mother's heart there's always room for one more.

Parental Payback

We've told our kids to never talk to strangers. But when the car pulls up, our children not only strike up a conversation, they hop right in. Then we realize the people in the car are only strangers to us. At least they are lately. A couple of decades ago they were telling us to eat our vegetables, clean our room and go to bed. We even referred to them as Mom and Dad.

Today, we're unsure of just what to call them...other than some bizarre, alien replicant of the parents who once ruled our home with an iron fist. And when our kids spend the night at their house, our folks only pretend as though they're doing us a favor. They maintain they're giving us some time to ourselves. What they're really doing is planting seeds of sedition.

When our kids ask for a bedtime story, our folks read it to them. Every word. They don't skip over pages and deliver the abbreviated version so they can get the kids into bed earlier. Dessert right before dinner? Sure. Seconds on ice cream, even when our kids are dressed in their Sunday best? You bet! As for those veggies, our folks don't even bother offering them to our kids. They claim that's our job. Right after Grandpa sneaks a lollipop out of his pocket and into the mouth of our youngest child. At 7 am.

Do you think that when these now-strangers bring our kids home over-tired, hopped up on sugar, lugging all of the toys we told our kids they couldn't have, that our parents don't have an ulterior motive? Think again. Our parents may call what they're doing "grandparenting." But we know better. It's payback. And we're on the receiving end.

The good news is it's a game we'll get to play soon enough. We just have to wait our turn.

If becoming a grandmother was only a matter of choice, I should advise every one of you straight away to become one.

Hannah Whitall Smith

It is as grandmothers that our mothers come into the fullness of their grace.

Christopher Morley

Being pretty on the inside means you don't hit your brother and you eat all your peas– that's what my grandma taught me.

Lord Chesterfield

*A grandma's name is little
less in love than is the doting
title of a mother.*

William Shakespeare

*In order not to influence a child,
one must be careful not to be
that child's parent or grandparent.*

Don Marquis

*Uncles and aunts, and cousins,
are all very well, and fathers and
mothers are not to be despised;
but a grandmother, at holiday time,
is worth them all.*

Sarah Willis

Little Gestures of Love

Mom: the ultimate social planner and hostess. She's the keeper of memories, the lighter of birthday candles, the stuffer of Thanksgiving turkeys and cleaner-upper of countless celebrations. She'll decorate, shop, wrap and bake. She can remember birthdays, favorite colors and who does NOT want nuts on their sundae.

But, it's the little gestures of love where moms really have a chance to shine. The lunchbox love notes. The impromptu slumber party during a thunderstorm. The invitation to head out for ice cream after a rough day at school.

As adults, which childhood memories will our kids cherish most? It may be the unplanned moments, the times they felt beyond the shadow of a doubt they were loved. By leaving a little wiggle room in our schedules, opportunities for simple celebrations will be more than a passing thought. They'll become a cherished memory.

*A happy childhood is one of
the best gifts that parents have
it in their power to bestow.*

Mary Cholmondeley

*What the heart has once owned
and had, it shall never lose.*

Henry Ward Beecher

*A mother's happiness is a beacon,
lighting up the future but reflected
also on the past in the guise of
fond memories.*

Honoré de Balzac

*Home is where the great are
small and the small are great.*

Author Unknown

A picture memory brings to me:
I look across the years and see
Myself beside my mother's knee.

John Greenleaf Whittier

God Bless all the Moms.